MADE EASY PRESS

# 101 INTERESTING FACTS
### about CHRISTMAS

*Stocking Stuffer*

**Fun and Festive Facts About the History, Traditions, and Culture of Everyone's Favorite Holiday**

Producer & International Distributor
eBookPro Publishing
www.ebook-pro.com

101 Interesting Facts About Christmas: Fun and Festive Facts About the History, Traditions, and Culture of Everyone's Favorite Holiday

Made Easy Press

Copyright © 2023 Made Easy Press
All rights reserved; No parts of this book may be reproduced or transmitted in any form or by any means, electronic or mechanical, including photocopying, recording, taping, or by any information retrieval system, without the permission, in writing, of the author.

Contact: agency@ebook-pro.com
ISBN 9789655753790

# INTRODUCTION

**It's the most wonderful time of the year!**

Ahh, Christmas. The lights, the food, the parties, the atmosphere — it is truly, the most wonderful time of the year.

But how much do you really know about Christmas? Do you know how tall the biggest Christmas tree is? Which president was the first to celebrate Christmas in the White House? Or which state was the last to make Christmas celebrations legal?

In 101 Interesting Facts About Christmas, you will discover all this and more!

So snuggle up by yourself or with the whole family and get ready to make the holiday season much more magical.

About 35 million live trees
are decorated in the U.S. every
Christmas and 50 million in Europe.

**Nanotechnologists in Glasgow created a minuscule Christmas card that is half a million times smaller than a regular-sized Christmas card.**

Santa's village in Canada is open for visitors every day of the year.

Gingerbread houses were inspired by candy house featured in the Grimm Brothers' fairytale, Hansel and Gretel.

# 8

Charles Dickens wrote "A Christmas Carol" in only six weeks.

The most common holiday injury is caused by falling off ladders and stools while putting up decorations.

In the Twelve Days of Christmas song, if you add up all the gifts, you will have 364 gifts - one for each day of the year, except for Christmas.

✦

**Recycled Christmas trees are sometimes placed in ponds to provide shelter for fish.**

✦

# 12

Mariah Carey wrote "All I Want for Christmas Is You" in only fifteen minutes.

**Christmas pudding was initially a soup made with raisins and wine.**

The busiest shopping days in the year are the Friday and Saturday before Christmas.

Some parts of a Christmas tree, including the needles which contain vitamin C, are edible.

# 16

Some zoos collect old, donated Christmas trees to use as food for their animals -- particularly the elephants.

In Sweden, it is traditional
to watch Donald Duck cartoons
on Christmas Eve.

**The first Christmas tree decorations were fruits, nuts, and candles.**

Children in Wales celebrate Calennig, where they walk around the neighborhood holding a decorated apple and singing carols, and get money or candy from their neighbors.

## 20

The world's tallest snowman was over 120 feet tall.

The U.S. government has issued Santa Claus an official pilot's license.

UPS delivers about 20 billion cards and gifts during the holiday season.

**Christmas Eve and Christmas Day are the two most popular days of the year for people to get engaged.**

# 24

The biggest gingerbread house ever constructed was big enough to live in.

The star of Bethlehem that guided
the wise men is believed to be
a comet or the planet Uranus.

The first U.S. state to recognize Christmas was Alabama. The last was Oklahoma.

Europe's largest and oldest Christmas market is held in Nuremberg, Germany.

The abbreviation "Xmas" comes from the Greek letter X, which is the first letter of Jesus' name in Greek.

In Home Alone, the ugly photo of Kevin's brother's girlfriend is actually a boy because the director thought it would be cruel to make fun of a real girl.

The most expensive Christmas tree was constructed in Abu Dhabi and was worth over $6 million. It was adorned with gold and jewelry.

Christmas trees are grown in every single one of the US's fifty states.

"Jingle Bells" was originally called "One Horse Open Sleigh" and was actually written for Thanksgiving.

The shape of the candy cane
is meant to represent "J"
for Jesus.

In Japan, it is traditional to have KFC for Christmas dinner.

President Franklin Pierce put the first Christmas tree in the White House, in 1856.

Then, in 1901, President Roosevelt
banned Christmas trees
from the White House.

The first Elf on the Shelf was called Fisbee.

38

The world's tallest cut Christmas tree was 221 feet tall.

In Ethiopia, Christmas is celebrated on January 7th.

Around the holidays, animal cracker boxes are sold with a string to hang the crackers up on the tree with.

There is a specific postal code
in Canada for letters to Santa -
HOH OHO.

**42**

For 13 years, between 1647 and 1660, Christmas was banned in the UK after the English Civil War.

Candy canes originated in Germany.

Hallmark holiday movies take on average just two weeks to shoot.

Santa Claus would have to travel over 200 million miles to deliver presents to all the children around the world.

# 46

Every year, a competition is held in California called the "Surfing Santa", where surfers dres as Santa to raise money for children with autism.

"The Grinch" is the highest-grossing Christmas movie of all time.

In India, people decorate banana or mango trees instead of traditional Christmas trees.

**Illinois has a Santa Claus parade that has been running yearly for over a century.**

# 50

The word "mistletoe" means "dung on a twig" - not so romantic.

Tinsel used to be made out of real silver.

The first donation to Toys for Tots was a handmade doll.

The Statue of Liberty was
a Christmas gift from France
to the US.

54

In Iceland, there is a Christmas tradition of giving books as presents on Christmas Eve.

During World War II, the playing cards
company Bicycle created decks
of cards with secret maps on them
and then distributed them to American
prisoners of war in German camps
to help them escape.

Sweden celebrates Christmas with a giant Yule Goat made of straw.

Tom Hanks is the voice of six different characters in the movie "The Polar Express".

# 58

Rudolph the Reindeer was almost named Reginald.

In World War II, German and British soldiers stopped fighting for a whole day to celebrate Christmas together, sing carols, exchange gifts, and play soccer.

The world's largest snowball fight involved 7,681 participants.

Spider's webs are a traditional
Polish Christmas decoration.

62

In 2012, Reddit organized a Secret Santa game with 30,000 participants.

The word "Noel" comes from the ancient Latin word, "natalis", which means "to be born". The words used to refer to Christmas carols, not the holiday itself.

The average American family spends about $1,000 on Christmas gifts every year.

Santa's red-colored suit was
partly inspired by a Coca Cola
advertising campaign
in the 1930s.

The record for the fastest time to decorate a full-sized Christmas tree is 36.89 seconds.

The holly of a Christmas wreath
represents Jesus' crown
of thorns.

The red, green, and gold of
Christmas decorations represent
the blood of Jesus, his eternal life,
and his status as king of kings.

The term "white elephant gifts",
meaning funny but useless gifts, comes
from the white elephants of Asia which
are considered very valuable
but completely useless.

Candy canes were originally straight white sticks, and only got their red color and curved shape later.

Modern Christmas ornaments are inspired by the shape of an apple, which were traditionally used as decorations.

**There are hundreds
of different recorded versions
of "Silent Night".**

The famous Rockefeller
Christmas tree features
over 25,000 little lights.

In Hungary, Santa Claus is called Mikulás, in Brazil his name is Papai Noel, and in Japan children call him Hoteiosho.

Christmas wasn't always celebrated on December 25th - the actual date of the birth of Jesus is lost to history.

The first-ever artificial Christmas tree was a German tree made of dyed goose feathers.

**Christmas trees grow for an average of 15 years before they are cut.**

The first ugly Christmas sweater party was supposedly held in Vancouver, Canada.

The word "Carol" means a song or dance of joy and praise.

# 80

**The day after Christmas is officially national candy cane day.**

Dry Christmas trees spark about 100 fires in the U.S. every year.

**The first artificial Christmas tree was made by a company that manufactured toilet brushes.**

Linus Urbanec from Sweden holds the record of the most Brussels sprouts eaten in one minute - 31.

84

A sugar plum is a candy made from fruit (usually plums) rolled in spices and coated with chocolate or sugar.

The world's largest gingerbread house was over 60 feet long and used over 8,000 pounds of gingerbread dough.

There is a town in Indiana called "Santa Claus", and another in Idaho called simply "Santa."

In Venezuela, it's a tradition for people to roller-skate to church on Christmas morning.

Edward Johnson invented
the first electric tree lights
in 1882.

A lot of families have a tradition where
they hang a small pickle ornament
from the Christmas tree and
the child who finds it gets to open
their presents first.

In Italy, children believe that an old witch named "La Befana" delivers presents instead of Santa Claus.

The Beatles hold the record for the most Christmas No. 1 hits, with four.

# 92

**Before turkey became a staple, a traditional British Christmas dinner featured a pig's head.**

In Scandinavian countries, holly
is called Christ Thorn.

Brazil has a massive Christmas tree that floats on water in Rio de Janeiro.

**Around the holiday season, almost 30 sets of Lego are sold every second.**

Saint Nicholas was a Christian bishop who gave away much of his money to help the poor.

A traditional Christmas dinner in Armenia consists of fried fish, spinach, and lettuce.

It took three hours every day to do Jim Carey's makeup for The Grinch movie.

Hallmark's Christmas cards have been in rotation since 1915.

# 100

**The biggest elf gathering ever was held in Bangkok, Thailand, and boasted 1,762 people dressed as elves.**

King William I of England was crowned on Christmas Day of 1066.

Every year, Oslo, Norway donates
a Christmas tree to the UK to be
placed in Trafalgar square in London,
in gratitude for the UK's help
during World War II.

The original "Rockin' Around the Christmas Tree" was sung by 13-year-old Brenda Lee.

104

In 1980, the most popular
Christmas gift was
the Rubik's cube.

Thank you so much for reading 101 Interesting Facts About Christmas!

I hope you enjoyed reading and learned some things you never knew about everyone's favorite time of year.

We'd appreciate it so much if you would consider going to Amazon and leaving a review.

Your reviews help us bring you more fun, family-friendly content like this book.

## ABOUT MADE EASY PRESS

At Made Easy Press, our goal is to bring you beautifully designed, thoughtful gifts and products.

We strive to make complicated things – easy. Whether it's learning new skills or putting memories into words, our books are led by values of family, creativity, and
self-care and we take joy in creating authentic experiences that make people truly happy.

Look out for other books
by Made Easy Press here!